THE FABULOUS LOST & FOUND

AND THE LITTLE MOUSE WHO SPOKE HEBREW

WRITTEN BY MARK PALLIS
ILLUSTRATED BY PETER BAYNTON

NEU WESTEND
— PRESS —

For Natalie - MP

For Hannah and Skye - PB

THE FABULOUS LOST & FOUND AND THE LITTLE MOUSE WHO SPOKE HEBREW
Copyright text © 2020 Mark Pallis and Copyright images © 2020 Peter Baynton

First Printing, 2020
ISBN: 978-1-913595-02-9
NeuWestendPress.com

THE
FABULOUS
LOST &
FOUND

AND THE LITTLE MOUSE WHO SPOKE HEBREW

WRITTEN BY MARK PALLIS
ILLUSTRATED BY PETER BAYNTON

NEU WESTEND
— PRESS —

In the middle of the big city is a tiny
yellow building. If anyone loses anything, this is
where it ends up.

It is called the Lost and Found.

Mr and Mrs Frog keep everything safe, hoping that someday every lost watch and bag and phone and toy and shoe and cheesegrater will find its owner again.

But the shop is very small. And there are so many lost things. It is all quite a squeeze, but still, it's fabulous.

One sunny day, a little mouse walked in.

"Welcome," said Mrs Frog. "What have you lost?"

"אִבַּדְתִּי אֶת הַכּוֹבַע שֶׁלִי" said the mouse.

Mr and Mrs Frog could not speak Hebrew. They had no idea what the little mouse was saying.

What shall we do? they wondered.

Maybe she's lost an umbrella. Everyone loses an umbrella at least twice, thought Mr Frog.

"Have you lost this?" asked Mr Frog.

"מִטְרִיָה? לֹא." replied the mouse.

Then Mrs Frog remembered something
that had been handed in a few months ago...

"Is this yours?" Mrs Frog asked, holding up a chunk of cheese.

‎"גְּבִינָה? לֹא. זֶה מַסְרִיחַ" said the mouse.

"Time to put that cheese in the bin dear," said Mr Frog.

"Maybe the word 'כּוֹבַע' means coat," said Mr Frog.

"Now where did I put that nice yellow one?"

"Got it!" said Mr Frog.

"מְעִיל? לֹא, אִבַּדְתִּי אֶת הַכּוֹבַע שֶׁלִּי" said the mouse.

She was starting to feel a bit frustrated.

"We need to keep trying," said Mrs Frog.

לֹא צָעִיף.

לֹא מִכְנָסַיִם.

לֹא סְוֶדֶר.

לֹא מִשְׁקְפֵי שֶׁמֶשׁ.

לֹא נַעֲלַיִם.

"אִבַּדְתִּי אֶת הַכּוֹבַע שֶׁלִּי!" said the
mouse.

לֹא שְׁנֵי אוֹפַנַּיִם.

לֹא מַחְשֵׁב.

לֹא שְׁלוֹשָׁה סְפָרִים.

לֹא אַרְבַּע בָּנָנוֹת.

לֹא חֲמִשָּׁה מַפְתְּחוֹת.

It was no good. A fat wet tear rolled
down the mouse's cheek.

"How about a nice cup of tea?" asked Mrs Frog kindly.

"אֲנִי אוֹהֶבֶת תֶּה, תּוֹדָה" replied the mouse. They sat together, sipping their tea and all feeling a bit sad.

Suddenly, the mouse realised she could try pointing.

"‏כּוֹבַע!" she said,
   pointing at her head.

"I've got it!" exclaimed
Mrs Frog, leaping up.

"A wig of course!" said Mrs Frog.

"לֹא פֵּאָה" said the mouse.

לֹא אֲדֻמָה.

לֹא בְּלוֹנְדִינִית.

לֹא חוּמָה.

לֹא סַסְגּוֹנִית.

לֹא יְרֻקָה.

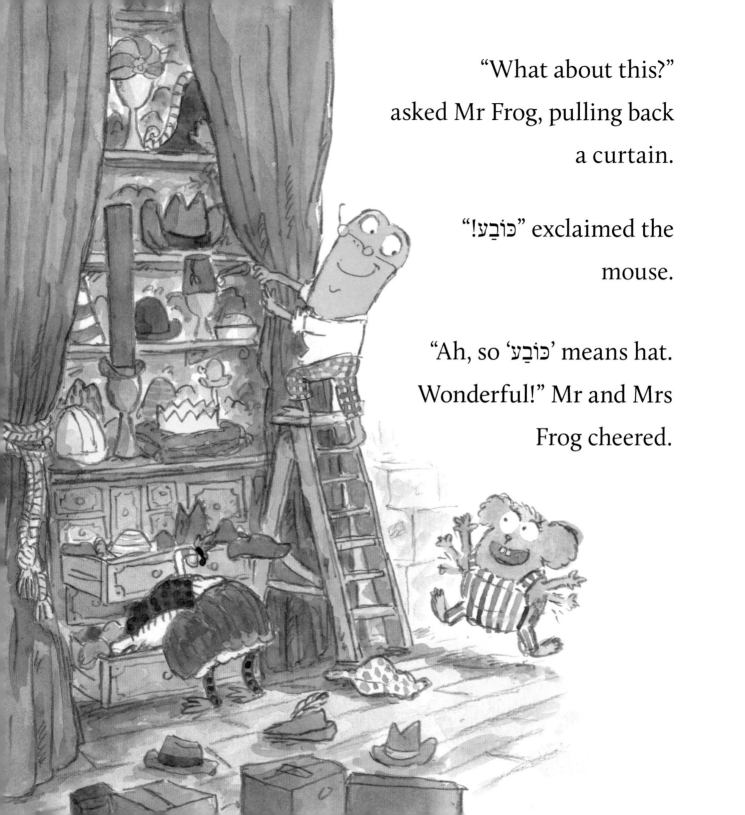

"What about this?" asked Mr Frog, pulling back a curtain.

"כּוֹבַע!" exclaimed the mouse.

"Ah, so 'כּוֹבַע' means hat. Wonderful!" Mr and Mrs Frog cheered.

גָּבוֹהַ מִדַּי.

קָטָן מִדַּי.

גָּדוֹל מִדַּי.

מָתוּחַ מִדַּי.

"One hat left," said
Mrs Frog, reaching all
the way to the back of the
cupboard.

"It couldn't be this
old thing, could it?"

"הַכּוֹבַע שֶׁלִּי! מָצָאתִי אֶת הַכּוֹבַע שֶׁלִּי! תּוֹדָה רַבָּה" said the mouse.

And just like that, the mouse found her hat.

"לְהִתְרָאוֹת" she said, as she skipped away.
"לְהִתְרָאוֹת" replied Mr and Mrs Frog.

"I wonder who will come tomorrow?" said Mr Frog.
Mrs Frog put her arm around him.

"I don't know," she replied, giving him a squeeze,
"but whoever it is, we'll do our best to help."

LEARNING TO LOVE LANGUAGES

An additional language opens a child's mind, broadens their horizons and enriches their emotional life. Research has shown that the time between a child's birth and their sixth or seventh birthday is a "golden period" when they are most receptive to new languages. This is because they have an in-built ability to distinguish the sounds they hear and make sense of them. The Story-powered Language Learning Method taps into these natural abilities.

HOW THE STORY-POWERED LANGUAGE LEARNING METHOD WORKS

We create an emotionally engaging and funny story for children and adults to enjoy together, just like any other picture book. Studies show that social interaction, like enjoying a book together, is critical in language learning.

Through the story, we introduce a relatable character who speaks only in the new language. This helps build empathy and a positive attitude towards people who speak different languages. These are both important aspects in laying the foundations for lasting language acquisition in a child's life.

As the story progresses, the child naturally works with the characters to discover the meanings of a wide range of fun new words. Strategic use of humour ensures that this subconscious learning is rewarded with laughter; the child feels good and the first seeds of a lifelong love of languages are sown.

For more information and free downloads visit www.neuwestendpress.com

איבדתי את הכובע שלי	I've lost my hat
מטריה	umbrella
גבינה	cheese
זה מסריח	it stinks
מעיל	coat
צעיף	scarf
מכנסיים	trousers
משקפי שמש	sunglasses
סוודר	sweater
נעליים	shoes
אחד (m), אחת (f)	one
שניים (m), שתיים (f)	two
שלושה (m), שלוש (f)	three
ארבעה (m), ארבע (f)	four
חמישה (m), חמש (f)	five
מחשב	computer
ספרים	books
מפתחות	keys
בננות	bananas
אופניים	bicycles
אני אוהב תה	I love tea
תודה	thank you
פאה	wig
אדומה	red (f)
בלונדינית	blond (f)
חומה	brown (f)

ירוקה	green (f)
ססגונית	multicoloured (f)
כובע	hat
גבוה מדי	too tall
גדול מדי	too big
קטן מדי	too small
מתוח מדי	too tight
מצאתי את הכובע שלי	I've found my hat
תודה רבה	thank you very much
להתראות	goodbye

THE WORLD OF
THE FABULOUS LOST & FOUND

THIS STORY IS ALSO AVAILABLE IN...

FRENCH
SPANISH
ITALIAN
CZECH
WELSH
KOREAN
GERMAN
GREEK
SWEDISH
POLISH
SLOVAKIAN
VIETNAMESE
LATIN
PORTUGUESE

...AND MANY MORE LANGUAGES!

ENJOYED IT?
WRITE A REVIEW AND
LET US KNOW!

@MARK_PALLIS ON TWITTER
WWW.MARKPALLIS.COM

@PETERBAYNTON ON INSTAGRAM
WWW.PETERBAYNTON.COM